Dear Janice, I be your
Always
ver

MW01001940

THE ONLY
JOB SEARCH
BOOK YOU WILL
EVER NEED

Thank you for
Supporting my 1st
Book.

Best Regards,

Curtis

Dear Laurie
Always strive to be your
very best!

Thank You for
Supporting my 1st

THE ONLY JOB SEARCH BOOK YOU WILL EVER NEED

Using The Marketing Mix To Rise Above Competition

Curtis L. Jenkins

Published by
Mynd Matters Publishing
715 Peachtree Street NW
Suites 100 & 200
Atlanta, GA 30308

ISBN-13: 978-0-9989323-0-9 (pbk)
978-0-9989323-1-6 (ebook)

FIRST EDITION

Cover Design by Digiecovers

CONTENTS

Preface 7

Chapter 1: Get Moving, Take Action.................................. 15

Chapter 2: Using the 4 P's of Marketing to Sell Yourself.... 33

Chapter 3: Product Development in Action 45

Chapter 4: Getting the Right Price for You as a Product 77

Chapter 5: Are You in the Right Place or Position? 97

Chapter 6: Promotion – By Others 87

Chapter 7: Putting the 4P's Into Action –
            Setting Goals For Your Future 111

Chapter 8: Pay It Forward: Success Stories 121

A Final Note 131

Acknowledgments... 133

Appendix 1: Questions to help you with your 4P's........... 137

Appendix 2: Summary of Actions.................................... 139

Appendix 3: Websites Useful to the Job Seeker 144

Appendix 4: Personality Types – Myers Briggs 145

PREFACE

THIS BOOK IS FOR YOU.

If you've spent the last one, five, or ten years filling out applications and sending fruitless resumes that receive no response, this book is for you.

If you've been on the job search for a long time and your confidence is shaken, this book is for you.

If you're a professional, or you're on the road to becoming one, this book is for you.

If you're searching for a soul-fulfilling career with upward mobility, this book is for you.

If you're climbing the executive ladder, this book is for you.

If you're an extrovert, introvert, or somewhere between the two, this book is for you.

If you're mid-career (management or not) this book is for you.

If you need a new job, a new career, or a systematic

method to meet your professional goals, this book is for you.

There are hundreds of articles and self-help books out there that repackage the same generic advice in different forms. They all tell you to take the same basic actions with slightly differing emphases. "Be early." "Do extensive research." "Master the art of the follow-up email."

Stop me if you've heard this before.

However, this book is different.

It is intended to be a quick read that gives you a sense of my job seeking journey through my stories and the lessons learned and put into action. In the next 20,000 words, I'll show you how to market yourself with the same techniques major companies use to sell products every day. You will shun the concept of clock-punching and shift your focus to utilizing your skills to provide value to employers, so they provide value in return. You'll discover how to leverage confidence, no matter what your personality type is.

To understand these concepts, you'll need to put aside

every assumption you've ever made about job searching and career progression. Some of these techniques will make you feel uncomfortable because they're the opposite of what you hear from hiring managers, or may seem to be outside your comfort zone.

The proof is in the results, though. I have seen this methodology work for countless people: outgoing and shy, wealthy and poor, formally educated and high school dropouts. This book was built for anyone and everyone willing to put one foot in front of the other.

If you're ready to do the work, read on.

COFFEE WITH BILLIONAIRES

Take a moment and envision your dream career benefits.

Do they include vacation time? A bigger paycheck? The ability to work from home? What about the opportunity to grab a drink with some of the most brilliant minds in your field?

There are two single elements that will get you what you're looking for.

The secret is a combination of **confidence** and **competence**.

I emphasize confidence throughout this book. In the job hunt, your potential employer is buying you and the skills you bring with you. Nothing makes an employer feel more grounded in their hiring decisions than seeing that you have confidence in yourself.

Confidence represents 80% of what employers seek in candidates. It cannot be gained when you play it safe. No matter your professional background or personality traits, confidence is a universal concept that grows when you take bold actions. You are in competition with others because there are always more people than there are jobs available, especially as you move up in your career. The actions in this book will outline building confidence, prepare you to sell yourself, and remove any lingering self-doubt stopping your forward momentum.

Competence is a wheel that never stops rolling. In order to climb a career ladder, you must constantly be learning, growing, and applying your knowledge. If your co-workers see that you're competent, they will collaborate with you—and having good professional relationships is the key to moving into better positions. If your boss believes you are competent, you'll be handed more responsibility and bigger projects. Most of us are very competent with the skills we have gained over our careers and lifetimes but are easily shaken if we lose a job or have been out searching for the right position for a long time. The actions in this book will show you how to hone and leverage your skills to become more appealing to employers.

WHY IS THIS THE ONLY JOB BOOK YOU'LL EVER NEED?

The genesis for this book began with a plea from a family friend whose husband desperately needed a job. She was aware that I had gained employment quickly after being laid off a few years prior. I wrote a seventeen-page summary of my personal daily job-hunting process, including some of the bolder moves I made to favorably position myself, and personalized it to fit her husband's needs.

Little did I know, this summary would be the basis of the most fulfilling work I've ever done. In the time since I typed out those first pages, I have had the opportunity to coach hundreds of job-seekers from all walks of life. Melding my personal experiences with theirs, I've created a system to help career seekers find employment, set goals, and get paid what they deserve.

As a project management executive, I've managed portfolios valued at more than $200 million. I've sat with, interviewed for, and presented to heads of multibillion-dollar companies. I've created a network of brilliant leaders, whose brains I have leaned on and learned from throughout the years.

This life-altering system is a culmination of these experiences. What I'm about to tell you is the most *results-oriented* and *confidence-building* process I have ever encountered. It is a replicable system that will help you stay employed, move financially and emotionally ahead, and shift your time and energy to finding joy in your career.

It is a system that will aid you in bouncing back from failures. Action leads to change, change leads to opportunity, and opportunity leads to the development of yourself and others. Once you learn how to build your personal brand and find the confidence to exhibit yourself as the best possible product, you will never be without job opportunities again.

This system has touched hundreds of lives. My goal is to touch millions of lives by sharing my process. As you take the actions described at the end of each chapter, the opportunities you dream of will materialize.

For those who are just starting in your careers – do not be discouraged as this book will be a handy reference for you to grow with as your career blossoms.

So, are you ready to change your future?

Let's jump in!

CHAPTER 1

GET MOVING, TAKE ACTION

"Never put off 'til tomorrow what you can do today." —Thomas Jefferson

THE BREAKING POINT

It was the epitome of a mid-career crisis.

On a brisk Tuesday in February 2002, I was called into an emergency meeting at the Student Finance Corporation in Wilmington, Delaware, where I was the director of project management. The purpose of this meeting was to discuss a second and final round of layoffs—a round which would include me.

I survived an initial round of layoffs a week earlier, so I wasn't shocked when I got the call. Surprisingly, management assured us that there would be no more layoffs at the earlier meeting. I assumed I could move on with my job as planned and begin to create the Project Management Office–the position I was hired for just six weeks prior.

When the dust settled at the end of the meeting, I learned that I was one of the casualties of the layoff. When the initial shock wore off, I was terrified. I joined a group of colleagues at a lunch meeting to talk about what just happened but couldn't keep my mind on their conversation.

This news would devastate my wife and two teenage boys. I couldn't go back to the job I had abandoned at BankOne a few weeks before. I had left abruptly, negotiating a resignation without reimbursing the $80,000 in tuition my former employer had paid for my Executive Master's degree. In exchange for the tuition, I was required to stay with the company for at least two years after graduation. Although I had been with them for a total of five years, I resigned only six months after graduating because I saw no prospects for career growth. The CEO agreed to the premature separation because he liked the idea of me being in charge of my *own* career path. Still, at the time, it seemed like a life-altering job move.

Well, the move was life-altering, but not in the way I would have ever expected. I burned my bridges and I needed a path to another job—fast.

"ARE WE GOING TO BE POOR?"

I called my wife and told her the news. We agreed to have an initial meeting to decide how we would explain things, and then sit down with our children. I wanted to gauge her reaction to my unexpected unemployment to see how anxious it would make her. I was relieved she was only slightly worried and was able to keep her fear from showing. It had only been eight weeks since I resigned from my previous job without consulting her; she was still upset with me. I hadn't turned in my resignation until securing the job at Student Finance, but she was still concerned about having to repay the tuition money. Luckily, I had it in writing that I would not have to repay $40,000 (one-year tuition reimbursement) since I completed a full year of work after my graduation in 2001.

We sat down with our two boys who were 13 and 15 years old at the time. They listened intently as I explained that Student Finance had lost the money for my position and put me on the chopping block.

My youngest son's eyes widened. "Does that mean we are going to be poor?" he asked. He was devastated, even though he didn't understand the concept of being truly poor. I'll never forget the look on his face or his question. It became the fuel for me to take visible action so my entire family could take comfort and learn from this experience. I knew the road ahead of me might be long, but I needed to forge ahead.

DEVELOP A ROUTINE – MAKE FINDING A JOB YOUR JOB

The next day, I woke up petrified. After tossing and turning all night, I was exhausted and anxious. I laid in a fetal position worrying about what my next steps should be. I knew I had to do something, especially in the light of my son's reaction. I didn't want my family to worry. After an hour, I mustered the strength to get up, declaring that my "mourning period" was over. I would no longer focus on the death of my previous job but on the birth of a new one.

The first action I took was to develop the plan and methodology of my job search. I took a shower and got dressed in a suit and tie, just as I always did when going to work. I went to our basement office and began browsing Monster.com.

I did the same for 6FigureJobs.com (which is now known as Ladders.com). I spent the entire first day scouring the internet for jobs. When my wife came home, she was surprised to see me looking as though I had gone to work that day.

The next day I also applied for jobs on the internet, but this time I also looked for career fairs and any other network-related gatherings. My weekly job-hunting routine was shaping up:

1. Get up and get dressed for work.
2. Search the internet until noon.
3. Spend 1:00 p.m. to 8:00 p.m. going to career fairs or networking events

After a few days, I added two additional items to my routine. First, noticing that conventional applications invariably generated nothing but the empty "We received your application" boilerplate email, I revamped my job application process.

I remembered a friend who got his job by submitting a proposal he developed for running a division of a company. I asked him for a copy of his proposal so I could draw inspiration from it. I wanted to effectively communicate why I was the best person for whatever job I was applying to. I developed a business case that I could modify to suit any opening. After several iterations, and with support from my friend, I crafted a business case/proposal template that was ready for the marketplace.

Eventually, my daily routine became:

1. Get up and get dressed for work.
2. Search the internet until noon.
3. Spend 1:00 pm to 4:00 p.m. taking my business case to several companies to get directly to the hiring manager.
4. Spend 4:00 p.m. to 8:00 p.m. going to career fairs or network events

Please understand this was *not* easy. In 2002, security at companies was very tight because of the September 2001 terrorist attacks. I often ran into security guards whom I begged for a chance to call either HR or the person listed on the job site. Out of every ten attempts, I usually was able to get three people who would meet with me and accept my proposal. I remember one of the managers saying, "Wow! I have never seen anyone this bold before."

* * * *

Showing up unannounced may not be the best move for you, depending on the culture of the company you're approaching and your own personality. This was also more than a decade ago. The job market has undergone some major changes since the 2008 financial crisis, and with the rise of online-only job applications, hiring managers are increasingly protective of their applicant search process.

In short: It was a gutsy choice, and most hiring managers didn't appreciate the effort, even then. Despite failing much more than I succeeded, it was one of the best learning experiences I've ever had. I would say that this was my first real foray into sales and the process of prospecting, cold calling, and trying to sell myself even before I understood sales and marketing techniques.

If you do take this approach, remember a few things:

1. **Over-prepare.** From the perspective of a hiring manager or executive, there is nothing worse than wasting time on someone who appears unqualified. This is why they have people fill out applications in the first place—to weed out

those who aren't qualified. If you show up and demand someone's time on the spot, make sure you know exactly who you want to talk to and exactly what you want to say.

2. **It doesn't take an extrovert.** For an extrovert like myself, being bold and direct comes easily. I know that I am an extrovert by definition and through my Myers Briggs Type Indicator (MBTI), I recently tested as an ESTP, however, during the time I was having this experience, I tested as an ENTJ. Maturity and circumstances have changed my overall outlook and view to my approach to life and career. The common thing on both tests is the E = Extrovert for me. However, if you tend to be more introverted, don't count yourself out so quickly. First, figure out what the root of your fear is. One of my more introverted colleagues told me she frequently opts out of gatherings and networking events with people she doesn't know because small talk is completely exhausting to her. Her alternative solution is to network through one-on-one lunches. If showing up at someone's office unannounced

leaves you feeling panicked, create a good rapport with the person you want to interview with beforehand. Comment on their blog or LinkedIn posts, shoot them a message with a career-related question, or retweet them. It's a lot easier to approach someone who at least knows your name than an absolute stranger. Figure out how your personality fits, employing the actions I suggest throughout the book. *Details of the MBTI are listed in the appendix.*

3. **Failing=Learning.** I'm OK if I fail or don't get what I want because I play the numbers game; just like a successful salesperson. Each time I fail, I gain an experience that brings me closer to success. Having the courage to fail over and over, without getting discouraged, is a lesson you can apply to almost every area of your life.

A PIVOTAL MOMENT

After three weeks, I still hadn't found a job, but I persevered. I felt good and my family was hopeful something would materialize. I signed up for a class given by 6FigureJobs.com and learned some of the very techniques and principles described in this book. With some refinements based on current trends in job seeking, these are the principles that I still use to this day:

1. **Create business cards** and have one ready for any occasion.

2. **Use the PAR (Problem – Actions – Result) or STAR (Situation – Task – Actions – Result)** method for your resume.

3. **Update your resume once a week** to keep it refreshed. That way, each week it is at the top of the search as headhunters seek candidates. Most people call within two days after your resume is posted.

4. **Validate** your intention to make job seeking a full-time job every time you leave the house.

5. **Remember** that hiring managers are interested in WIIFM: *What's in it for me?* In this regard, hiring managers base their selections 15% on technical ability and 85% on fit, chemistry, personality, confidence, and trust.

6. **People are willing to pay** a very high price for

confidence. Remember, you're selling yourself.

7. **Placing a "career objective"** at the top of your resume sends the wrong message. It is counterproductive. Career objectives are candidate-oriented (what I want), and not customer-oriented (what the hiring manager is looking for, or WIIFM).

8. **Remember that the HR/Personnel Departments are not the best contacts for job seekers.** Bypass HR personnel whenever possible. Deal directly with the hiring manager or someone several levels above the vacant/targeted position.

9. **The best time to interview is Thursday afternoon or Friday morning.** This is the "Pizza Box Effect." They have seen the rest, now they will see the best (at last).

10. **Follow up aggressively.** After every interview, remind them you're the right person for the job.

I can't emphasize how much value I took from a class that only cost $55. I've talked to an enormous amount of unemployed people who were hesitant to pay $55 to invest in their future. Any serious job seeker should understand hiring professionals if they expect to be paid by them. I've found most individuals who benefited from my advice and counsel were the ones who paid me. I know some people are motivated by free advice, as I am one of these individuals, but if I find that I need to pay an expert to achieve my goal, I will pay to get that advice. The form the advice comes in or how you get it don't matter as long as you get it, and follow the teachings!

* * * *

Once I had established a consistent daytime routine, that varied only as needed to attend the occasional job fair or class, I began to add new elements to my evenings. I would, for instance, search for networking venues focused on my discipline (Information Technology). I saw an article in the newspaper for a meeting held by the Black Data Processors Association (BDPA), a nonprofit organization founded in 1976 focused on creating opportunities for minorities in IT.

I then went to said meeting and met both the local and national presidents, as well as other members of the organization from chapters across the country. The mission of the organization was a great fit for me and my values. I had admired this group of professionals for their work in the community and for their personal accomplishments. I immediately joined the organization, agreeing to pay dues of $75 a year. I asked the President of the Philadelphia Chapter,

"What is the one thing you need now that would make the biggest difference to the organization?"

Her reply was that she needed a person to run the monthly program meetings, set up the topics, reach out to potential speakers, and ensure events were well planned and executed. Without hesitation, I responded,

"Search no more; I'm your guy!"

Soon after, I was voted in by the Philadelphia chapter's executive board as the Vice President of Professional Development and went to work immediately for the organization.

I soon added an additional element to my evening routine. I began systematically informing my acquaintances that I was unemployed. Most of us don't want to let our friends and professional network know we have lost a job; we feel that unemployment is shameful. I took the opposite approach. I told everyone I could think of that I was looking for a job. Before I went to bed, I would develop a list of ten people to email, call, or visit. Occasionally, I employed all three of these methods on the same person. My idea was to establish and enlarge a network to help me look for work.

This is an especially good approach for those who struggle when networking with complete strangers. Catching up with old acquaintances over time, especially online, can be much less taxing than attempting to create brand new relationships.

After four weeks of following this routine consistently, I met an enormous amount of people, learned an incredible amount of information about the job market, and became a lifetime member of a great organization. And yes, I also landed a job. The offer was the result of a phone call to a former coworker, who was interested and kind enough to speak to the head of the Project Management office of Fleet Credit Card Services. I submitted my resume and was immediately scheduled for an interview. After the initial set of interviews, a follow-up interview was arranged with the head of the department. I got the job.

My success was attributable to a series of factors: my network, a great series of interviews, and a thank-you letter template which included a 3-page proposal for hiring me (a touch that showed my originality and credibility to my interviewers).

CHAPTER 1 ACTION ITEMS

1. **Reject Shame.** Do not be ashamed of losing your job. The job market is not what it used to be, and things change quickly. Let everyone know what you are looking for and enlist them in your search for the next opportunity. Most employers incentivize their workforce to help bring in talented new employees. This creates a win-win situation for everyone.

2. **Apply for unemployment.** Don't be ashamed. I hated those long lines and the entire process, but I had to do it. It helped me and my family enormously.

3. **Develop a routine and refine it as required.** My

routine does not have to be your routine, but it gave me and my family the confidence that I would eventually find a job. It seemed as if I hadn't been laid off, because I made it my job to be looking for a job.

4. **Pay for what you need to get what you want.** If you really need it, the benefits outweigh the cost. Paying for instruction guarantees you will try to absorb the information you are provided so that you can apply it effectively to your job search. Studies show our brain is more positively affected from gains that we worked for versus gains given to us.

5. **Step out of your comfort zone.** Do things to be noticed. You can be unique without being distracting. I once saw a news story of a man who wore a sandwich board with his resume on it. I don't know how that worked out for him, but years later, I can still recall the sight of this unemployed man trying to be noticed. This was an extraordinary action that I will never forget. If you struggle to be bold, more subtle gestures (such as speaking on ideas, issues, and personal passions that excite you) can leave a huge impact. I will never

forget a quiet subordinate who was able to convince me of an idea that she thought would make a difference for the company. She was unable to convince us all collectively but stepped out of her comfort zone and passionately explained her idea in detail. When I fully understood her impassioned idea, I became the vehicle to help push it through. The result was both accretive results for the company and an above-average rating and promotion for her.

CHAPTER 2

USING THE 4 P'S OF MARKETING TO SELL YOURSELF

"Don't sell life insurance. Sell what life insurance can do." —Ben Feldman

THE 4P'S OF MARKETING

Before we discuss marketing yourself as a product, let's first discuss the 4P's of marketing so that you understand the basis of the Marketing Mix. The Marketing Mix is a term originally formulated by Neil Borden and refined by E. Jerome McCarthy. Both the Marketing Mix and 4P's are designed to compartmentalize a product's unique selling points that differentiate it from competitors.

The 4P's of Marketing—Product, Price, Promotion, and Place/Position—is a model for enhancing the way you take a new product or service to market. It helps to define your marketing options, so your offering meets a specific customer need or demand.

It's simple. You need to create a *product* that a group of people want, put it for sale in a *place* people visit on a regular basis, *price* it at a level commensurate with the value they feel they get out of it, and *promote* it at a time they want to buy.

A lot of work needs to go into finding out what "customers" (companies you'd like to work at) want and where they do their "shopping" (recruiting). You also need to figure out how to produce the item (you) at a price that reflects its value to the customer (your salary) and get it all to come together at the critical time.

If just one element is wrong, it can spell disaster. It's the equivalent of promoting a car by highlighting its amazing fuel economy in a country where gas is very cheap or publishing a textbook after the start of the new school year.

The questions I often ask clients in relation to these principles are:

1. **Product** – What are you selling? What are you very good at? Can you articulate it? It is imperative you have a clear grasp of exactly

what your product is and what makes it unique before you can successfully market it.

2. **Promotion** – How is your brand/image? What do people say about you? Are you trustworthy, reliable, and dependable? Promotion is the way marketing agencies disseminate relevant product information to consumers and differentiate a product or service. Promotion includes elements like advertising, public relations, social media marketing, email marketing, search engine marketing, video marketing, and more.

3. **Place** – Are you in the right place in terms of business, profession, industry, and position? Often you will hear marketers say marketing is about putting the right product, at the right price, in the right place, at the right time. It's critical to evaluate what the ideal locations are to convert potential clients into actual clients. Today, even in situations where the actual transaction doesn't happen on the web, clients are initially engaged and converted online.

4. **Price** – What value do you bring? Do you know how much you are worth in the market? Similar (in concept) products and brands may need to be positioned differently based on varying price points. You must know this to negotiate the best salary for yourself.

CONFIDENCE IN YOUR COMPETENCE: THE 4P'S AND YOUR PERSONAL BRAND

Whether you like it or not, you have a personal brand. I began to really understand my own personal brand from a book I read called *Lions Don't Need to Roar*. I have always been fascinated by lions in general for their fearless nature, majestic look, and strong familial ties to their pride. I like lions so much that my company logo has one in it. When I saw the title of the book, I understood it immediately. A lion does not have to roar, but you will always respect a lion because you know of its capabilities. After reading the book, I understand even more that how I carry myself is like my own personal book title. That is one of the reasons I wear a suit or jacket most days, and why people notice it when I don't have one on.

YOUR brand is a combination of your in-person and

online image. People perceive you in a certain way, whether you've tried to control your reputation or not.

What do potential employers find when they Google you? What do people say about you as a person and a professional? What are you known for? Is your brand detrimental to your job search? Does your personal brand exemplify what you're trying to sell?

I once told a CFO "I sell confidence" and he laughed. Working with a limited budget, he had been assigned by the CEO to get major processes in the company under control. After he and I discussed the problems and organized the work into manageable projects, I asked him how he felt. Was he confident to tell his boss he had the answers and knew how to implement the program? He replied, "Yes! And you are absolutely right—you *do* sell confidence!"

It doesn't come easily. I spent years molding a reputation and convincing people I know what I'm talking about. I put in the work to earn my face time with the CEO and CFO. I earned my position by performing and promoting my personal brand. It was this brand that encouraged my boss to promote me and place/position me in situations where I could perform my craft at the highest levels of the company.

If you want to sell competence you must be confident in your product—your ability to organize work, use your personal skill set, and apply leadership to drive execution. You also need the confidence that you can articulate this valuable skill in a way that "customers" can understand.

"But Curtis, you're a natural extrovert! Even thinking about 'selling myself' or my skills makes me feel sick."

I can't tell you the number of times I've heard some variation of this line. While it's true that I'm a gregarious people-person, I have **many** self-proclaimed introverted friends who are very successful. Leadership and confidence are not exclusive to one personality type. Anyone can lead in their respective industry by proving they are **competent.**

Susan Cain, author of the book *Quiet: The Power of Introverts in a World That Can't Stop Talking*, says it best:

"The secret to life is to put yourself in the right lighting.

For some, it's a Broadway spotlight; for others, a lamplit desk. Use your natural powers—of persistence, concentration, and insight—to do work you love and work that matters. Solve problems. Make art, think deeply."

In other words, it's not about what your skill set is as much as how you can use that skill set to provide value. You must brand yourself as an expert in whatever you do. Become a leader in your industry:

- **Publishing**—Put content on major platforms such as Medium and LinkedIn. Reach out to online and physical niche-specific magazines to see if they would be willing to publish an article on trends in your industry.

- **Connect online**—Get a branded Facebook page (not just a personal one). Answer questions related to your field on Quora and Reddit. Make sure you have a personal website set up. Establish your online brand so you show up when people are Googling information about your field.

- **Be a one-on-one mentor**—Sharpen your

leadership skills by mentoring someone new in your field.

- **Let your work speak for itself**—Just because you're not the loudest person in the room, doesn't mean your work can't be. Promote yourself by showing that you can finish projects creatively, on-time, and without problems.

- **Take every opportunity to speak in public**— This doesn't necessarily mean you need to speak to an audience of thousands, but any occasion you have to vocalize your personal brand is a good one. Consider speaking in a local chamber of commerce meeting, as a guest in a local community college class, or even to a troop of boy/girl scouts.

EXCEL IN YOUR STRENGTHS

In the book *The Tipping Point*, author Malcolm Gladwell describes three kinds of people: Connectors, Mavens, and Salesmen.

A **Connector** is someone who knows large numbers of people and who enjoys making introductions. They have friends and acquaintances within many social, cultural, and professional circles. They tend to link these circles together thorough events, references, and general conversation.

A **Maven** is an "information specialist" who is always gathering facts, figures and context. They tend to accumulate knowledge and know how to share it with others to help solve problems.

A **Salesman** is a persuader, often born with powerful negotiation skills. They tend to have charismatic traits that make others want to agree with them.

Every workplace needs a balance of people with different, natural skills. You don't need to (and won't) perfect all these traits. It's more important and efficient to focus on which traits you naturally have and work on exemplifying them within your line of work.

While your core personality doesn't change, it's also important to realize that you may undergo shifts in how your skills are displayed in your job/position and how those shifts are perceived. When I started my career, I came across as a Maven. I was constantly trying to fix issues and troubleshoot problems. As time went on, and I took on leadership responsibilities, my natural ability to connect people became evident. I found that it was always there, I just didn't fully utilize it until later in my career.

Recognize and capitalize on your natural talents. The better you understand yourself, the more you'll be able to promote yourself as a product. In essence, looking for a job is an act of sales, recruiting is negotiation, and hiring is buying/closing the deal. Sell your strengths, no matter what they are.

CHAPTER 2 ACTION ITEMS

1. Read and understand the 4P's of Marketing

2. Make sure that you can answer these personal marketing questions:
   - Product – What are you selling?
   - Place – Are you in the right place, business, profession, industry, and position?
   - Promotion – How is your brand/image built? What do people say about you?
   - Price – What value do you bring?

3. It will be very helpful to write the answers down

and check to see that they are clear.

4. Continuously refine the answers to these personal marketing questions while on your job search. Don't wait for the perfect answer to your personal marketing questions. Keep refining them even after you get a job.

CHAPTER 3

PRODUCT DEVELOPMENT IN ACTION

"Know your enemy and know yourself and in 100 battles, you will never be in peril!"
—Sun Tzu, The Art of War

For businesses that use the 4P's, the Product refers to a good or service a company offers. A product should meet a certain consumer demand or be so compelling that consumers believe they need it.

Believe it or not – in the job market, you are a product that companies are looking to buy. They trade your time with the money they pay you. Therefore, companies want to be certain that they are buying the best product at the best value.

Before a potential employer meets you, they already have an idea of who you are. This is because they've already looked at your resume, LinkedIn profile, googled you, checked your social media, or spoken to others about you. Yes—hiring managers, interviewers, and human resource departments do their research too! Take control of things like your social media presence, your resume, and other elements that represent you when you are not present to represent yourself.

SCRUB YOUR SOCIAL

Social media was in its infancy when I began my job search in 2002. Social media platforms for networking and job searching such as Facebook, Twitter, and LinkedIn didn't exist. Because almost all companies now use social media for recruitment and referrals, you must ensure that your online profile is complete, professional looking, and free of spelling and grammatical errors. Not being careful about your profile on social media will severely handicap your ability to find employment.

Of all the social media sites, LinkedIn is my preferred tool for connecting with and building my network. I am careful not to post anything in my profile that I wouldn't put on my resume.

CREATING A SIX-FIGURE RESUME

Getting your resume in shape is key, even if you haven't searched for a job in a while. Remember, you are not the same person you were one, five, or 10 years ago. Your resume should reflect that growth.

When I began my job search, my resume did not accurately reflect my capabilities or notable accomplishments. It wasn't even formatted attractively. When I'm working with people on their resumes, I often have people tell me that their goal is to get a job paying six-figures. When I hear this, I ask them directly if they think their resume justifies a six-figure income. They almost always answer "no."

All resumes show what has been done in the past, but most are deficient because they show only job responsibilities while ignoring the opportunity to show value by describing the results of their experience. During my class at 6FigureJobs.com (Ladders), I learned to write my resume with the PAR method – *Problem, Action, Result.* The key advantage of this method is that it allows the job seeker to show their potential employers quantified results. These metrics also give a sense of the magnitude and scope of your work, the resources you managed, and the ways you can be of benefit to the company.

Below is an excerpt of my resume before and after I revised it based on learnings from the 6FigureJobs.com class.

2000 Resume:

First USA Bank – Delaware

Jan 2000 – Present   Project Manager

Data warehouse Project Manager – Data Rationalization Project. Develop savings in cost avoidance by rationalizing enterprise data. Recognize data duplication and process synergies and execute by capacity constraints, data model and data changes, aging off data with hierarchical storage methods and reporting using decision support systems. This project is ongoing with short– term savings realized as they are recognized. Longer– term projects are staffed and planned with milestones. Develop and report Cost– Benefit Analyses and present savings to the executive sponsors.

July 1998 – Dec 1999   Project Manager:

Responsible for development and support of several ongoing and new marketing initiatives. Duties include working directly with the users for full lifecycle development, standardization, and data warehousing initiatives. Determining scope and business requirements with the users. Managing development, testing and implementation. Resolving all issues concerning the project. Hiring personnel, managing career development, and performance appraisals. Technologies of these projects include: Oracle (embedded SQL and PL/SQL), Visual Basic 5.0, UNIX, Windows 95 and NT environments, Pro*C, SAS, Micro strategies.

Received promotion to Assistant Vice President.

First USA Bank – Delaware
May 1997 – July 1998   Client Server Developer:
Developed PL/SQL scripts to extract information in Oracle Databases for data analysis of existing credit cardholders. Work with DBA's to set up DB links to outside vendors to share output. Setup automated scripts using UNIX cron to FTP data across secure T1 lines.
Created Random Number generation package in Oracle. Used company– wide for "seed" programs.

2002 Resume after Ladders class:

BankOne*, Wilmington, Delaware · 1997– 2002
A leading banking and financial services corporation.

Application Developer/Oracle Database Programmer/Project Manager
Earned Service Awards and 2 promotions to Project Manager and Assistant Vice President as a result of delivering key strategic projects.

Key Results & Accomplishments:

- **Realized over $1.2M annual operating expense** return by completing e–mail consolidation project from 10 disparate platforms to a single platform.

- Completed major frame relay network and infrastructure project, which included **a team of over 50 IT professionals and coordination with 9 business partners.**
- **Negotiated multimillion-dollar contracts with IBM and AT&T.**

*BankOne purchased FirstUSA Bank in 1997 but was not noted in 2000 resume.

The length of the resume was cut in half and the revised version includes powerful examples of my contributions to my previous organizations. It shows that I made a very positive impact on the business and brought much value as an employee. Because technologies change so rapidly, it is more important to emphasize the ways your work improved the business than your proficiency in a specific technology at a specific time. This is especially crucial for IT professionals, who are often perceived as obsessed with technical jargon and technology for technology's sake. It is imperative that all job seekers emphasize their contributions to the strategic goals of the organization or to the processes that all businesses employ.

ADDITIONAL TIPS FOR BUILDING YOUR RESUME

- **Delete the "objective" statement.** At best, most objective statements say nothing about an applicant and at worst they are redundant. For example: "Seeking employment as a CPA to leverage my professional expertise and grow into an accountancy role within your company." You're already applying for an accounting job, so isn't this a given?

- **Supply contact information for your references** and never say, "References furnished upon request." This phrase is suspicious on its face, implying that (good) references may not exist. At a minimum, it is annoying to the potential employer who has to waste time asking for what should have been supplied in the first place.

- **Write a summary** but write it last in order to ensure you have captured the essence of your completed resume. Executive summaries for business cases are written this way. Your resume is a business case for hiring you.

- **Make sure the information is up to date and**

relevant to the job you are applying for. Your McDonald's job right out of high school doesn't matter when you are a 20-year project management professional.

- **Make sure you have a neutral email account.** Something like [FIRST NAME], [INITIAL], and [LAST NAME]. Example: CJenkins@ emailplatform.com. Do not use an email address which is immature or unprofessional. Even though this seems like a miniscule detail, your email address is an extension of your personal brand. Think about it this way: What does batmanrocks2014@yahoo.com really say about your judgment?

REPRESENTING YOURSELF AS A PRODUCT WHEN INTERVIEWING

Now that you have your resume and social media presence buttoned up, you may have been lucky enough to score an interview. This is the most meaningful interaction and could make or break the entire engagement. I will purposely spend a lot of time on this section because of how important it is. This is the opportunity to represent yourself through several forms of communication. Think of this like online dating, if you've ever tried it. You made an intriguing profile to garner interest, and eventually you went from talking on the phone to hopefully going out on a date. There is no guarantee of chemistry, but each person is putting their best foot forward. This goes for face-to-face encounters, networking events, and more. If you are prepared to be "interviewed" in various forms, you are prepared to engage anyone in your career aspirations.

There are numerous do's and don'ts for interviews. I won't take time to go through obvious points such as being on time, being well groomed, and so on. These are the basics for any interaction with other people. Always ensure that you are presenting your best professional self.

Instead, this section will cover various types of interviews, how you should prepare for an interview, what to do while you are being interviewed, and the actions you should take post-interview.

TYPES OF INTERVIEWS

The four most common interview types are:

- Individual (hiring manager, HR person, non-hiring manager, or peer)
- Group (hiring panel)
- Phone
- Video

I like to connect with an interviewer and establish a rapport. Before you set foot in someone's office or in front of a camera, make sure you understand as much about who your audience is and what they're expecting as possible.

The individual interview: Make sure that you answer the questions that you are asked. As an interviewer, it is irritating when someone gives me a response that does not answer my question. When this happens, sometimes I give the interviewee the benefit of the doubt and rephrase the question to ensure I am being clear. If you are unsure of the question, please ask the interviewer to repeat the question, or repeat it yourself as a preface to your answer. Be sure to maintain eye contact and answer questions clearly and truthfully while still putting yourself in the best possible light.

The panel interview: My advice for the panel interview

is the same as the individual interview, albeit with one significant difference: you must address each member of the panel while simultaneously making sure that you include the senior panel member in every response. Analyze the power dynamics in the room to identify the decision maker or the person with the most influence. This person is usually the senior manager or the hiring manager. You can recognize the decision maker by eyeing who the other people in the room look at when they speak. This isn't to say you should ignore the other panel members. On the contrary, whenever anyone asks a question, be sure you look at the questioner when you begin your response. While you are providing your answer, try to make eye contact with each member of the panel, especially the senior member, making sure to end your response while looking at the person who asked the question. You will know you are doing well when everyone in the group mirrors each other with head nods, smiles, and laughter.

The phone interview: The sometimes-necessary evil. Phone interviews are often used for a quick screening of candidates, and in this capacity, they can be very useful. I can remember once wishing I had phone screened one candidate who walked into an interview and said, "I don't know why I am here; I don't know anything about software development." I was so mad! Although this candidate was a company referral, her resume was plagiarized, and she didn't know anything about software development. It was a complete waste of time.

- Make sure your responses are very clear. Your voice should convey confidence and control. To do this, stand while speaking and open your lungs as if you're addressing a group; your voice will sound commanding and clear over the phone.

- Be ready with stories centered on your resume and your accomplishments.

- Have a concise summary of the company's information in front of you. You should tailor your stories and your answers to emphasize their relevance to the company. To do this, I often pin a summary of the main points about the company on the wall and glance at it as I recount stories and answer questions. This has often resulted in my being asked to come into the office for a face-to-face interview.

Phone interviews tend to be shorter than individual or panel interviews, although the same general considerations apply. Remember to ask for clarity whenever you're unsure. Finally, make sure the phone interview is not affected by your need to take a bathroom break!

The video interview: Video interviews seem to be the wave of the future, as technology allows us to communicate and collaborate remotely. A Skype interview with the ability to see and interact with the interviewer is preferred. A "canned video interview," on the other hand, is a video of a person reading a series of questions into the camera that you're tasked with responding to. No one else is in the video, and all interviewees get the same video. It can be pretty impersonal. I once took a canned video interview, recording my responses as a response to a video of someone asking questions. I didn't like hitting the "reply" button to answer questions from an unknown person I never got the chance to meet.

During a canned video interview, you can add the human element by asking someone to stand in front of you and hold the device you're using. This helps you feel as if you're interacting with a person face-to-face—allows you to project your best self.

PREPARATION

It is very important that you prepare for an interview as far in advance as possible. However, once you have mastered the preparation techniques I am about to describe, you will need increasingly less prep time because you will always be prepared for spur-of-the-moment formal and informal interviews. Each engagement scenario with professionals is an opportunity to market your capabilities to a potential employer.

BEFORE THE INTERVIEW

Learn everything there is to know about the company, the industry, and the person(s) who will interview you. If there is a panel, ask for their names ahead of time so you can gather information about everyone. This is an *action that you must take to stand out from other applicants.* Fortunately, there are many internet services or sites, including the company's own website, where you can easily find the information you need.

I usually focus on the key items I need to know to understand the company. This includes news affecting the company that I can cite to make my questions and comments more thoughtful. The base information I study in preparation is:

- The company's business: what they do to make money, business delivery models/verticals
- The company's statistics: annual sales, financial information, number of employees, locations
- The company's culture: creed, mission, vision, and values
- Industry news: big acquisitions, mergers, or new law/regulations that are applicable
- Trends: movement in the industry, growth and product fads that affect the performance of the company, or related products and services

To understand the people who will interview you, you'll need their names, positions, and an understanding of the things that are important to them. Social media is a great source of this sort of information in the absence of a mutual friend, acquaintance, or colleague willing to provide such insights. I find that the most useful social media platforms for gathering professional and social insights are LinkedIn and Facebook, respectively. I also like to do a quick internet search for anything written by or about the person I'm preparing to interview with.

It is also important to develop a rapport with your interviewer. In *How to Win Friends and Influence People*, Dale Carnegie explains that getting a job is simply influencing someone to hire you. He says you should arouse an "eager want" in the interviewer. One way to do this is to speak to their interests. Hiring managers have a need, and you can portray yourself as the best candidate by answering questions from the others person's point of view. Framing your responses from the employer's perspective helps them to see how you can fulfill their needs.

Finally, you must know yourself. For the interviewer to get a better understanding of you, they will most likely ask you one or more of the following questions:

- Tell me about yourself.
- What are your strengths, weaknesses, or challenges?
- Why do you want the job? What interests you

about the job?

- Why are you the best-qualified person for the job?
- Why did you go into this line of work?
- What do people say about you? Boss? Peers? Subordinates? Customers? Suppliers?

You need to be authentic as you answer these questions. Practice the answers until you have honed your message to a fine point, speaking clearly and succinctly.

The most crucial decision companies make is in the hiring and firing of employees—this is your time to shine!

GET YOUR STORIES STRAIGHT

Behavioral interviewing is a technique in which the applicant is asked to describe past behavior in order to determine whether he or she is suitable for a position. Research shows behavioral interviewing is approximately 55% predictive of future on-the-job behavior, while traditional interviewing is only 10% accurate. Behavioral interviewing, more than other interviewing techniques, provides a more objective set of facts on which to make employment decisions.

Behavioral interviews essentially boil down to storytelling. You are asked questions that reveal your technical capacity, including your attitudes toward the work, team members, and superiors. A typical question in a behavioral interview begins, "Tell me a time when..." My approach is to have a few well-rehearsed stories that can be used, with slight variations, to answer such questions. With only a handful of stories, you can address items such as:

- A time when you had to report bad news
- A time when you influenced peers, superiors, customers, and suppliers
- A time when you had to deal with conflict
- A time when you made a serious mistake and what you did to handle it
- A time when you had a difficult customer
- A time when you negotiated a solution that benefited your company
- Your ability to work with a team
- Your ability to adapt and or effect change in an organization
- Your successes and failures

These are only a few examples of behavioral questions that I have encountered. You can have one main story which can often be adapted to focus on the answer to each of the questions. Practice your stories and responses with someone to ensure you are using the most effective words while telling the story as succinctly as possible. End each story on a positive note, highlighting the lesson you took from the experience.

In preparing for an interview, I find it useful to create a table that provides an outline of my accomplishments and projects, as well as the value they created for the organization. The table below is one that I created to reflect my experience.

Program/ Project	Budget	Resources/ Impact	Innovation	Value Created
Critical Infrastructure Protection Program	$7M	8/Departmental	Discovered inefficiencies within the K9 unit and recommended a commercial off-the-shelf solution for capturing and reporting K9 training and utilization.	Improved productivity by creating one-man year of capacity for one K9 unit whose primary job became capturing and consolidating spreadsheets and creating reports.
SAP– Global Transfer System Implementation	$2M+	10/Global	1. Transferred key responsibilities and deliverables to the Logistics Team – IT to focus on technology, Logistics to focus on Change Management.	$40K per month consultant costs reduced by 50% to $20K per month, and project schedule reduced by 50% (2 months from 4 months).

			2. Reduced consultant hours (cost) to meet deliverables on time and on budget.	
Mergers & Acquisitions	$30M+	Varies by project/Global	Created M&A Playbook – Disciplined, easy to follow approach to deliver integrations quicker at best possible cost.	50% reduction in integration schedule. 40% reduction in costs to deliver greater synergies. Global SWAT team to reduce travel costs & increase local knowledge.
IT Budget	$29M (O) $10M (C)	25 Emp 100 Vendors & Contractors	$1.3M budget mistake – reduced employee salary costs, vendor costs, rationalization of tools	1. Reduced SGA costs towards corporate goals 2. Drove IT costs in line with benchmark costs (1.5% of sales to 1.2% of sales)
Program Management Office (PMO) Development @ 2 separate companies	$30M	25/Global	Created 7-step Project Management Delivery process to speed up delivery, while maintaining key project necessities for a culture that abhors bureaucracy and paralysis	1. Able to execute over 40 projects totaling $30M+ from demand to delivery in first year of company 2. Saved the company $24M in Transition costs by quickly executing separation from parent company

A table like the one above helps me to frame my interview responses using either the PAR (Problem, Actions, Results) or STAR (Situation, Tasks, Actions, Results) approach, the standard response formats for behavioral interviews.

Based on the job description, I put together no more than five major accomplishments that are relevant to the job. Each of them should uncover the types of behaviors the interviewer is looking for. In large projects, a few situations often arise that become great stories in the end. You should always look at these situations as opportunities while you are overcoming them. Conflicts or mistakes are opportunities for learning and growth; they become important lessons to draw on later in your career and your life.

As you'll notice, I list the situations in a grid. It starts with the program and/or project. You can also see this as the "problem," because every project or program should be a solution to a problem or problematic situation.

The budget, resources, and impact areas frame the magnitude of my responsibility in resolving the problem. These columns frame the problem and my scope of responsibilities, providing information useful in responding to secondary questions regarding my scope of responsibility relative to a specific project. The innovation section allows me to speak on differentiating actions that were taken, and the value created summarizes the results.

Do not memorize a table and regurgitate it verbatim to

an interviewer. Not only will they be bored stiff, but you will completely miss the point and the opportunity to be engaging will be lost! The value of the table is it facilitating quick recall of critical information, not providing you with a verbatim script for your interview.

AT THE INTERVIEW

Final preparation before the interview ensures you ask the interviewer(s) the right questions at the right time. This is crucial to understanding your limits and constraints, what is being asked of you and the importance of your answer, and having enough information for a great post-interview opportunity to sell yourself. Listed below are the questions *you* should ask during each interview-related interval.

1. Before you start the interview:

- How much time do we have for the interview? The answer tells you how much time you have to sell yourself.

- Is it okay if I take notes? Ask for permission to take notes/keywords to ensure you remember what is important to them – this helps you prepare a strong thank you letter. Please don't take notes while answering a question, only when you have asked a question. Also, don't write so much that you lose eye contact and engagement with the interviewer, as this will be a major turnoff.

2. During the interview:

- During the interview Q&A period, make sure you answer the questions succinctly – do not drone on with your stories. It is okay to ask if you have answered the question to the interviewer's satisfaction. Don't be afraid to ask to have a question repeated or rephrased, even if only to have a few more seconds to gather your thoughts.

- Always ask questions when the interviewer asks if you have any. Nothing impresses me less than when a candidate has nothing to ask. The smartest people are the most inquisitive people. Here are a few examples of questions you might ask (refer to Appendix 3 for a more complete list):

- o What is the most pressing issue facing the company today?
- o What are the common successful behaviors exhibited by your top performers?
- o What are the top three issues this position must solve – short term and long term?
- o I read your mission, vision, values, etc. Can you give me an insider's view of the company's culture and what the company does to cultivate it?

Make sure you have good follow-up questions so you appear to be interested. Ask every interviewer the same question to look for patterns or anomalies that you might be able to use to your advantage when selling yourself further down the road.

3. Immediately following the interview:

- • "May I have your business card?" Be sure to get the business card of the interviewer at the start of the meeting if possible. This will give you the opportunity to reinforce remembering their name and title along with their contact information. This is also important for a follow-up letter.

- If you have multiple interviews the same day, ask to use the bathroom after each one. Use this time to quickly touch up your notes so you can recall them more easily. Then check yourself and get to the next interview with a high degree of confidence!

DAYS AFTER THE INTERVIEW

After the interview, remember to follow up and thank everyone for interviewing you. The most common way of doing this is to send emails via company email or through a LinkedIn account. Personally, I don't respond to such emails or LinkedIn requests unless I am *sure* this is a colleague I want to have.

I like to provide my interviewers an email with a business proposal embedded in a thank you letter. Primarily, I do this to stand out without being overbearing or distracting. I also do it to assure the interviewers that I was paying attention to what matters to them (this is why you ask every interviewer the same handful of questions). Finally, I do it to increase the level of confidence and show I can solve their problems, using excerpts from my resume to remind them of the experience I have in solving just such problems.

Here is how I construct my proposal/thank you letter:

1. Executive Summary

Example: Thank you for the opportunity to discuss my past accomplishments for the [Position] role at [Company]. My future endeavors as a project manager include working within an organization where project management processes and principles are valued. I am working on my Project Management Professional Certification to enhance my leadership skills.

You expressed a few common themes during the interview. These themes included why [Company] is a great place to work, the characteristics of a successful candidate, and the major issues for the managers. In addition, there was a discussion on the characteristics of a candidate who is considered a senior project manager. I've attached a proposal addressing each of these themes, as well as the reasons why now is a great opportunity to obtain the services of the best available candidate.

2. [Company] is a great place to work – characteristics of the company overall

I gathered from our conversations that [Company] is a dynamic, aggressive, and smart company. These are all characteristics that I possess, a fact which makes me the best available candidate. *(selling points here and below)*

There are several reasons why I want to be a part of the [Company].

ComputerWorld has ranked [Company] in the top 10 as one of the best places to work in IT. You provide

- [Benefit 1]
- [Benefit 2]
- [Benefit 3]

Based on the Project Management Institute's definition of an organization, [Company]'s PMO is structured as a strong, balanced matrix organization. I work best within an organization with this structure because it provides the best opportunity to show the value of a project manager. I would be an ambassador for all current and future employees on the merits of working for [Company].

3. Successful Employees in [Company]

The following points emphasize the characteristics of successful people in [Company]. These characteristics are:

Strategic thinkers who see the big picture:

To improve work processes, I have developed a strategy to ...

To improve communications, I have developed a strategy to ...

People who take initiative for opportunities to improve:

To improve organizational communications, I created the ...

To save money and to improve operations, I ...

[Closing sentence on successful employees.]

4. Major Issues of [Company] Management

Are people engaged in what they are doing?

I have very good people skills for recognizing when a person ....

Do people see the big picture?

I am a strong advocate for big-picture thinking and I ...

Closing sentence on major issues of [Company] Management

5. Conclusion

Several times I asked about what makes a person suitable for additional responsibility and compensation, and the response was usually that the person needed supervisory experience...

In my experience I have ...

Experience #1 (Company or Job Title):
>   1– 3 bullets of supporting actions taken.

Experience #2
>   1– 3 bullets of supporting actions taken

[Concluding paragraph]

It may appear as a bit much, but it's been extremely

effective for me. I am currently a hiring manager, and I've only seen a proposal like this one time. It was for a cybersecurity position that I was interviewing candidates for. My boss and I were impressed by the proposal. The candidate submitted a rebuttal to our current architecture as he understood it from the interview questions that he asked. He went on to explain in detail how it would be beneficial to switch from our current path to another, more secure and cost-effective approach. We called this candidate's recruiter right away so that we would not lose him to a competitor. I know this works because I have used it successfully in every new company that I have worked for since 2002. In 2007, I built a similar proposal to create my own job within a company.

CHAPTER 3 ACTION ITEMS

1. Get your resume in order. Look at current examples of great resumes in your field of work. Have it reviewed by trustworthy and skilled colleagues.

2. Prepare for the interview like you would prepare for a huge test.

3. Practice interviewing with trusted colleagues, family members, mentors, sponsors, etc.

4. Develop a marketing proposal for hiring you and use it after the interview.

5. Always follow-up from interviews as you would do with any new potential relationship.

CHAPTER 4

GETTING THE RIGHT PRICE FOR YOU AS A PRODUCT

"Too many people overvalue what they are not and undervalue what they are." —Malcolm S. Forbes

Congratulations!

You've followed the process of developing and selling the best product/person for the job, and the company is going to make you an offer. Long before you get to this point, you should know what your price is, and what you're willing to agree on when accepting the position.

In the business context, Price is the cost consumers pay for a product. Marketers must link the price to the product's real and perceived value, and also consider other costs such as supply costs, seasonal discounts, and competitors' prices. For you, you must play the role of the marketer of you as a product, and show demonstrated value of your skills and offerings as an employee.

Have you ever asked yourself, *"What am I worth?"* Why are you worth this? Are you worth more? What evidence do you have that you are worth more? I will help you refine your answer to these questions. A solid understanding of your value as an employee is the most important piece of preparation you can have going into a salary negotiation. It will bolster your skills in confident, effective negotiation.

THE TOTAL PACKAGE

When preparing a response to an offer, or estimating your worth as an employee, you should concentrate on the *total compensation* for a job. Just before a company makes an offer, they usually inquire about your current salary. Beware that they do this to anchor you in the upcoming salary negotiation. Therefore, if possible, *do not disclose your current salary.* If nondisclosure is not an option, be sure to give them a figure that includes short-term and long-term incentives, benefits, and job-related perquisites in addition to your salary. The company already has a budget for the position, and they can either afford your price or they can't. I have turned down plenty of positions when my potential employer and I could not agree on a salary. In one instance, I declined an offer because of insufficient total compensation, only to be contacted by the same company twice in subsequent years. I found the attention flattering, but the compensation they could offer was still below my own estimate of the market value of the position they needed to fill. Be firm in your own compensation demands.

One way I prepare is to estimate my *researched value* and my *individual value.*

Researched value is a measure of what the market pays for a position. This is a key benchmarking exercise; you need to know what the market is paying for a specific position in your geographical location. To estimate researched value, I use **payscale.com**, **salary.com,** and **glassdoor.com.** All three are free and easy to use.

When you input the position you're researching, you also indicate a specific location. There may be some ambiguity in the title, so you may have to look at several similar-sounding positions based on the job descriptions. Once you pull up the results, look for the median value (top of the bell-shaped curve). This is what I consider to be my minimum position in a salary negotiation. However, I really am aiming for a salary between the 75th - percentile and the 90th - percentile. The figure below is an example of the output for salary for a project manager position in the construction industry from PayScale. Be sure to look at everything including bonuses, benefits, and salary to come up with a comprehensive view of total compensation.

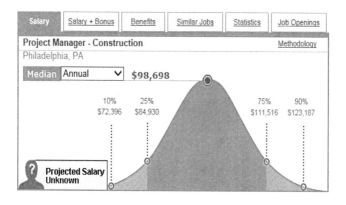

Be realistic about where you are in your career and on the bell-shaped curve. Also, location matters; you wouldn't want to accept a North Dakota salary for a New York City job. The tool is adjusted for cost of living in different locations across the globe. You should also realize that the data in these programs is based on people who chose to opt into surveys about their compensation. The positions described may not be identical to the position description of the job you are seeking or have. The information is crowdsourced but gives you a framework for your salary negotiations.

The **individual value** is what you use to separate yourself from the pack. This is what I use to justify my claim to deserving a salary in the 75 - 90 percentile. In making a case for my individual value, I typically use a combination of my past performance ratings, leadership experience, and relevant volunteer experience. I also like to bring in any stories I used in the interview or follow-up letter/proposal to remind them why they are considering me in the first place. Whenever possible, I also make use of my professional networks and affiliations to recommend additional hires for positions other than the one I am seeking. I have received many accolades for bringing in additional high-performing talent who provided value immediately after they themselves were hired.

Know your price; use your **researched value** to understand what your position is worth in the marketplace and make a value claim. Then use your skills, stories, accomplishments, and network to sell your individual value. By using both, you will be able to negotiate with confidence. Remember -- confidence trumps competence.

1. **Research your profession's salary range.** Check with recruiters in your field (even if you don't pursue their leads), as well as competitors, the U.S. Department of Labor's Occupational Outlook Handbook, the internet, your local chamber of commerce, and trade publications.

2. **Select a target salary or total compensation value.** You may not get the amount you want but having a specific target can help you get close.

3. **Don't initiate salary discussions.** Wait for the interviewer to bring up the subject, even if it's postponed to a second interview. It is tempting to bring this up too early. Don't! Once they are "interested" in you, you are in a better position to begin this discussion.

4. **When asked for your salary requirements, say that they're "negotiable."** Do the same on applications by writing "negotiable" in any box

asking about salary details. If the form asks you to provide current salary, write "to be covered during interview." This isn't being evasive, because you can't select a salary without knowing details of the benefits package. It is also a good idea to initiate a discussion about the position's salary range when asked for your salary/compensation requirements. If your request isn't granted, excuse yourself politely and leave. Would you want to work for a firm that won't or can't respond to this legitimate request?

5. **Discuss benefits separately from salary.** Your list of benefits can include insurance, tuition reimbursement, relocation payments, stock options, bonuses, and outplacement upon termination.

6. **Analyze all benefit packages.** Team up with a family member, close friend, insurance agent, or investment professional. They'll provide you with an invaluable second opinion and may help you look at the offer more objectively.

7. **Consider the cost of living.** Especially if you're

moving to a new area. If living costs are higher, suggest that you be paid a differential.

8. **Use examples of your accomplishments that prove your value, not merely your experience.** In discussing why you deserve a substantial increase, comparisons to your current salary are irrelevant and should be avoided. Focus on the benefits you'll *bring*, not your past salary, over which you may have had no control.

9. **Always assume a first offer is negotiable.** Never accept an offer at the interview! Express your strong interest, but state that you always discuss decisions of this magnitude with advisers whose judgment you have relied upon for years. Tell your interviewers when you'll contact them with your decision.

CHAPTER 4 ACTION ITEMS

1. Know your value based on research. Use available tools such as salary.com, glassdoor.com, and payscale.com to help you with your research.

2. Know your value based on your experience and accomplishments. Consult with peers/colleagues to

help you best express your value.

3. Study salary negotiations skills and techniques. Use the above list of nine points to help you.

CHAPTER 5

ARE YOU IN THE RIGHT PLACE OR POSITION?

"Opportunities don't happen. You create them."
—Chris Grosser

Another question I ask clients is, *"Are you in the right place?"* Imagine a supermarket shelf in the soup aisle where there are multiple options. Marketers fight to position their products at the eye-level, or "buy-level," of the consumer. Product location is one of the myriads of factors in the enormous amount of scientific research that goes into trying to influence consumers' decisions. Place decisions determine where a company sells a product and how it delivers the product to the market. The goal is to get products in front of consumers most likely to buy them. In some cases, this refer to placing a product in certain stores, product placement on a store's display, or where a product appears on a web page. But here, we are talking about *you* being in the right place or position at the right time. You must position *yourself* so that you can appeal to the buyer or, in this case, the employer/hiring manager.

This is also about being true to yourself. Mid-career, I had to face the fact that no matter how many different things I tried, I still loved and gravitated toward project management. This is because I love seeing a vision take shape, watching the assets being built, the growth of the team, and my personal development. Peter Drucker, who wrote *Managing Oneself,* stated that we are at our best when we are at the intersection of our strengths, values, and performance. The Self-Determination Theory, initially developed by psychologists Edward L. Deci and Richard M. Ryan, suggests that competency and mastery are nurtured when people are in positions that match their talents and desires. We are at our best when we are able to choose what, how, and when we do our work, AND when the outcome of our labor has a real impact on something important. The temporary nature of projects not only gives me quick satisfaction, but it also gifts me a variety of opportunities to move on to the next project and learn new things around new people while applying my skills.

The relatively temporary nature of projects doesn't mean that I don't continue to learn things that C-Suite leaders need. In contrast, I become more valuable to these leaders when I meet their project needs with tasks with fiscal responsibility, strategic planning, and strong talent development

Here's a personal story that illustrates the importance that education and corporate relationships play in enhancing our individual brand and positioning.

Completing the Executive Master's program at the University of Pennsylvania did not directly represent a path to a new job, but it did indirectly help my search by providing opportunities I would not have had otherwise It enhanced my competitive edge. I had to take two significant actions to obtain my Ivy League advantage. The first was to ask Randy Christopherson, the then-President of First USA Bank (my employer), and someone I saw at the gym occasionally, to support my application by providing financial support.

It all began when I read fragments of an article on a seatmate's newspaper during my afternoon train commute home. The article concerned the University of Pennsylvania's Executive Masters in Technology Management program, and it featured Mr. Christopherson, a supporter of the program since its inception in 1998. I noted that Mr. Christopherson was scheduled to speak at a program-related event the next weekend. After getting off at my stop, I immediately purchased that day's Wall Street Journal and took it to work the next day. I took the newspaper to the gym and had it with me when Mr. Christopherson came out of the shower with a towel wrapped around him. I said hello, and then showed him his picture in the article describing his support of the program and his upcoming speech. I then told him that I wanted to attend this program and went on to ask for the company's support in doing so. His response was, "Sure!" He then told me not to go to my direct supervisor, but to send a direct message to the CIO, who reported to him. Mr. Christopherson told me to say that he supported the company providing the financial support for me to attend the program.

I was startled by his willingness to support me, especially considering the fact our relationship was based on little more than saying hello to each other at the gym. He did ask about my performance reviews, and I told him I had earned consistently good ratings over the last few years. The next day, my supervisor was very upset with me; emails were flying back and forth about the support from the president, when I had not spoken a word to him about my aspirations.

The lesson I drew from this experience was to go directly to the top to preclude the risk of becoming stuck in the middle. I was asked by my manager and my peers what I had done to get such an opportunity. They wanted to know why I got special privileges when they'd worked just as hard. The answer I gave them is the same thing I tell everyone today: I asked! That's it; nothing magical. The worst thing that might have happened would have been being told no, and that was a risk I was willing to take.

I was prepared for the opportunity; it was one of the best things to happen to me from a career perspective, a relationship perspective (both social and corporate), and an educational perspective. A condition of his assistance was to submit to a series of interviews with all of the Senior VP's. This was also a huge opportunity because it provided me a lot of visibility and led to full corporate support for the program and my participation in it. Now I have an Ivy League resume stamp that separates me from other job searchers. I have relationships with top-notch colleagues who are eager to provide references, and I have close friends with whom I can learn from, travel with, and grow through.

GROW THROUGH YOUR MENTORS

Believe it or not, I've found most high-achieving people want to share what they know. They gravitate toward people who are intellectually curious; people who are interested in what they are doing. In other words, those who are higher than you on the career ladder **want** to share what they've learned in their journey and help you along yours.

This isn't to say that they'll help just anybody. Each of us has a finite amount of time in a day, and this is especially true with people who have been highly successful. Mentoring is certainly a give-and-take relationship.

The place you find yourself in is not as good as it could be if it does not allow contact with older, wiser, or simply more experienced practitioners of the kind of work you want. This is critical access to people with the unique power to get you noticed. Almost no one reaches the highest level of any profession without the coaching, constructive criticism, and nurturing of someone more experienced. You might consider a mentor to be a personal friend, post-graduate tutor, or life coach. A sponsor is more than a mentor, although they often do the things a mentor does. Sponsors are distinguished from mentors by the fact they put their own reputation on the line by proactively seeking out employers and recommending you to them.

Keep in mind there are always exceptions to the rule. There will always be people who are afraid of you, who feel threatened by you, and those who are generally insecure. I call these people scorpions because they are always on the defensive. They aren't willing to mentor you because they sense that they're losing something by sharing. Don't give these types of people a second thought--they are only capable of impeding your journey.

HIRING HELP TO BEST POSITION YOURSELF

In my career, I asked my successful friends if they ever hired someone to help them and I was shocked to find out that each of them had a career coach. Well, I'm one who follows paths of success, so I asked for references and finally settled on someone who I thought would be the greatest fit for my own journey. I hired a career coach whom I paid $150 an hour to help me navigate my career path toward the executive ranks. We would meet for an hour monthly and I would leave with homework. In the hours we spent together, I learned so many things that I could apply immediately after I left the session. From negotiations to understanding myself, it was the best money I've ever spent on my career. The return on my investment was enormous.

Another benefit of hiring my career coach was adding another person in my network who would always be an advocate and supporter of my future job search and career moves. You may have to invest more than time to gain a competitive advantage in the job market.

If a career coach is out of your reach, find a mentor who is 2-3 positions ahead of you in your projected career path. You'll find many people are willing to give an hour or two each month to guide your path and advocate for you, but you must be willing to reach out and ask. This advice to hire a coach is more for seasoned professionals as I did not take this action until after my mid-career layoff in 2002, when I was ready to get hired into an executive role like my successful friends.

Another benefit of hiring any professional is that they have access to *other* professionals. Your financial planner will have access to people who are in business and could introduce you. A career coach has access to others like you and can provide introductions, advice, and relatable stories which could help you with your job search or career aspirations.

Much of the advice in this book circles around the value that personal and professional contacts carry when obtaining a personally and financially rewarding job. This emphasis resurfaces here. If the place you find yourself in does not offer the same opportunity for personal promotion I found in the gym with Mr. Christopherson, it is not the right place.

My challenge to you is to find work that is personally meaningful. Only then can you work with your supervisors to match your skills to your position, as well as the tools and autonomy given to do your best.

Where do you want to work? Where have you been? Where do you want to be?

CHAPTER 5 ACTION ITEMS

1. How can you put yourself in a "buy-level" position? Look at your past and current positions – are you ready for a growth opportunity?

2. Ask for what you want. Determine what you want to do and ask people of influence to help you.

3. Develop a list of people who would be great mentors or, better yet, sponsors. Determine who can make introductions or sponsor you.

CHAPTER 6

PROMOTION – BY OTHERS

"Convert your fans into your customers by adding value to what you do." —Israelmore Ayivor

Promotion ties into the other three P's of marketing as promoting a product shows consumers why they need it and should pay a certain price for it.

In this context, I use Promotions as it relates to reputation development and maintenance, or in other words, having people who can promote you while you're promoting yourself. This helps the consumer, or hiring manager, determine why they need you and should they pay the price that you are asking for. Here is an opportunity for your network and references to help make that decision. Every time you engage with other people, judgements are being made about you, whether you like it or not. Luckily, you can control the narrative with each engagement that you have. These are the three questions I ask when it comes to someone's promotion:

1. Can your network get you where you want to be?
2. Do you have a big network of people that will promote your skills?
3. What do people say about you that you don't say about yourself?

Whenever I can speak to someone about career goals, I always ask a few questions about networking and business socializing. All too often, what I receive in response is a blank stare. I find this astounding! I want to ask such people how it is that they have *not* surrounded themselves with like-minded, progressive people who can assist them with their goals in life. We are surrounded by our peers, yet few of us have tried to deliberately use these interactions for mutual benefit. Remember, seeking a job *is* a job; it must be woven into your daily routine, both outside and inside the workplace, with friends and colleagues.

Networking and business socializing are very important components of career success. They can't be conveniently switched on and off when you do or do not need someone's help. If you become known as a person who shows up only when you need something, you'll find yourself on an island quickly. I tell people that I am searching for a job every day. In my behavior with my network of family, friends, fellow volunteers, and business colleagues, I always try to show myself as an expert in my field - someone who is trustworthy and able to get any job done. The people in my network feel a sense of satisfaction and pride when they promote me for positions. Almost every week I get calls from friends, family members, recruiters, headhunters, and former business colleagues about suitable business opportunities.

When I lost my job in 2002, references were not coming because I had not nurtured my network. At that time, I let key relationship opportunities fade away because I was caught up in less meaningful areas of my life. I was afraid that networking and business socializing would interfere with me spending time with my wife and children. I thought it would take away from the great experiences I was having. In hindsight, I know nurturing my networks would have enhanced *every* aspect of my life.

Identify people who can get you where you want to go, give you a great reference, and who you can help in return. These are the people you should weave into your life.

NETWORKING AND BUSINESS SOCIALIZING

Looking for a job is like looking for a partner. You want your network to serve as a "matchmaker" who can support you as the best available candidate. People are picky about choosing their mates, just as they are with finding candidates. Getting a referral from a trusted advisor gives comfort and confidence to the job seeker and the potential employer.

I like to ask my job search clients the following question: "Can the people in your life get you to where you want to go?" Over 90 percent of the time the response is no. I am amazed by this response, because our relationships are critical to finding opportunities at or near the top of the pyramid.

NETWORKING THROUGH VOLUNTEERING

Volunteer work is a tremendous way to grow your network. While volunteering, you have a huge opportunity to grow and learn while simultaneously advancing the values and issues you care about. You are spending time with like-minded individuals who have diverse skills and backgrounds and open themselves up to new relationships because of the shared values. The opportunity for practicing and developing a new skill through volunteer work cannot be overemphasized. If you want to learn something new, volunteer for a committee where your skill set is needed.

The way I learned how to run a business and manage a large budget was by joining the National Black Data Processors Association (NBDPA), which I did in 2002. The NBDPA is a nonprofit, tax-exempt organization consisting primarily of persons directly employed by or interested in the IT industry. In May 1975, Earl Pace, Jr. and David Wimberly founded the NBDPA in Philadelphia. They formed the group out of a shared concern that minorities were not adequately represented in the computer industry. It was the first national organization to address issues related to the "digital divide." The NBDPA provides professional and personal enrichment through monthly meetings and other activities. Education, skills training, and professional development programs are some of the strategies actively used by the association in reaching these objectives.

More than 15 years ago, I saw in a newspaper ad that the quarterly board meeting of the national board of directors was being held in downtown Philadelphia, and that new members were being solicited. I had heard about the organization and knew that they focused on people in the IT field. I went to the meeting and met some amazing and impressive leaders from across the country. I also met the President of the Philadelphia chapter, and was so excited by the work that they were doing in the community and the IT industry that I joined that very day.

But I did more than write out a check for the $75 membership fee; I immediately asked where I could help, and what opportunities there were for me to grow and contribute to the organization at the same time. I agreed to take on the position of VP of Professional Development. This position not only required me to refine my project management skills in the planning and execution of the monthly programs; it also allowed me to meet and develop relationships with industry leaders while forcing me to develop my (then rather limited) skills as a public speaker. I was able to practice all these things with no real risk. There was no performance appraisal outside of the praise for a job well done, and caring support when the job wasn't up to expectations. The boldest step I took in this position was the creation of a 13-month, forward-looking calendar covering topics of interest to the membership. This calendar advertised IT topics for which I found qualified industry leaders who had the time and willingness to speak on for free. This became the nucleus of a web of relationships that I maintain to this day.

Because of my success as VP of Professional Development, I was encouraged by NBDPA members and leadership to run for President of the Philadelphia Chapter. (I had by that time secured a position with Fleet Boston Financial—the first job I found after being laid off in 2002, a major sponsor of the NBDPA.) My election to this position catapulted my career because of the access it provided to Fleet's senior leaders, and how I was able to tie to it my role at NBDPA. Specifically, I had built into my performance plan the management of these monthly conferences as they related to Fleet's sponsorship, visibility, diversity and inclusion goals.

I have never had to actively look for a job since the day

I began my volunteer work with NBDPA. As President of the Philadelphia chapter, I had an opportunity to display my abilities over time, and to establish myself as a peer to the movers and shakers in my industry.

I have also seen other volunteers who lost the drive to perform as a NBDPA volunteer when they lost their job and had to focus on finding another. My advice to them, which probably seemed counterintuitive, was to work even harder in the organization. I told them this primarily because of the way they could use volunteerism to nurture and expand their career source network and their confidence in the things they can control.

The treasurer of the NBDPA during my tenure as President exemplified someone who failed to take advantage of the networking opportunities associated with volunteer work. When this person lost his job, he slacked off on his treasury duties, thereby disappointing the rest of the board which led to calls for me to replace him as quickly as possible. I spoke to him and expressed my disappointment over his failure to submit his reports on time. I told him about the demands for his replacement by the other members of the board. He explained his poor performance as the result of his being unemployed for two years. I replied that he was looking at it the wrong way, and that the real reason no one had hired him in two years was his demonstrated inability to keep his commitments. I also said that no one on the board would help him because of his unreliability. He had at his disposal CIOs and senior leaders who could have helped him with references, but he squandered these resources by failing to keep his commitments.

This conversation reduced the man to tears. But in the end, he and I reached an agreement. If he would refocus on his duties as treasurer and get the board behind him, I promised I would help him with his job search. Bottom line: he did refocus on his duties and he did repair the fractured relationships with the board. Within two months of his turnaround, we helped him find a job and provided positive references.

My current position was created by my friend, a colleague and Corporate Advisory Council (CAC) member. CAC is a board of advisors that I helped form to provide leadership and advice to the Philadelphia Chapter Board of Directors. In 2006, he asked me to be a part of his executive team. Remember: your relationships can be long lasting, but you must work at them, taking pains to demonstrate your worth when you can do so. Never lose sight of the fact that this is not a one-sided deal. There are many programs and incentives for people who can help their companies find great talent. Ask your friends and colleagues if their companies have referral programs. Filling positions by word of mouth is a win-win for everyone because of the huge savings in recruitment costs.

THE POWER OF NETWORKING

Below is a story written by the Digital Intelligence Systems Corporation (DISYS) to highlight the value of networking.

It happened again! The partnership between Sheila Black and Curtis Jenkins yielded yet another successful career move. Both are members of NBDPA Philadelphia Chapter and both are now working at Amtrak. Since 2002, Sheila and Curtis have helped each other secure employment by keeping in touch and nurturing their professional relationship through NBDPA related activities, including leadership by serving on the NBDPA Philadelphia Chapter Executive Board as President

(Curtis) and Vice President of Communications (Sheila).

In this latest round of opportunity, Curtis introduced Sheila to Kristin Trombulak, DISYS Account Manager for Amtrak, who was looking to fill a Technical Project Management position. As a result of her diverse project management experience and interviews, Sheila was awarded a job. Curtis Jenkins stated, "Sheila had the experience, and I knew if she got an interview that she would demonstrate her ability to secure the job. Creating the link between the talent and the need is what networking is all about." This created a win– win– win– win for DISYS, BDPA, Sheila Black and Curtis Jenkins.

Kristin Trombulak stated, "Referrals are so powerful that they can make your business succeed or not. This is why the power of referrals is so important to our business. You never know who is walking in to your client. A preliminary interview only covers so much, but a solid referral makes DISYS feel more confident. Amtrak was extremely impressed with DISYS's ability to fill such a demanding position in such a short time. Had DISYS not reached out to our current consultant base referrals, and had Curtis not reached out to his network of professionals,

I truly believe DISYS would still be recruiting on this position today[1].

People with strong networks get more things done and use their network to seek positive change in both their careers and during a professional crisis.

In building your network, please do not chase people. Everyone won't be receptive to being a part of your network, or being your mentor. Everyone won't see your value but be sure to remain confident that you *do* have value. Remember that this is a relationship and people need to be as attracted to you as you are to them. I have had many failed attempts at networking with specific people that I wanted to learn from or build a personal relationship with. However, when I realize that the relationship will not grow, I leave it alone. There have been times when a person that I originally wanted to have in my network was not receptive to the

[1] Digital Intelligence Systems Corporation (DISYS) is a global technology and business services consulting company that is known for its commitment to client satisfaction. Incorporated in 1994 and headquartered in Chantilly, VA, DISYS is a certified Minority Business Enterprise (MBE). The company is an information technology firm offering consulting, system integration, hardware/software sales and services, and mobile computing solutions. With offices and delivery locations spanning North and South America, Europe, and Asia Pacific, DISYS has earned a reputation for offering clockwork deployment, outstanding client service, and state-of-the-art solutions.

relationship sought me out to help at a later date. I would help them because that is the value that I bring. I was also told that if I was available, they would hire me.

The good news is that networking doesn't need to be a chore. It can be an enjoyable and rewarding part of one's professional development. Joining an organization related to your field allows you to learn from others and to demonstrate your expertise and experience. Once a member, you are building your skill sets and networking, while doing good for the community and society at the same time.

CHAPTER 6 ACTION ITEMS

1. Don't wait until you need a network before trying to create one. Start now, whether you are employed or not. Continue growing the quality of your network. List 10 people who can help you get where you want to go. Create a social way of connecting such as coffee, lunch, mutual hobbies, etc.

2. Attend network events and actively seek out the right people for mutually beneficial relationships.

3. Assume a highly visible position of authority with an affinity group/association. Make sure the group matches your passion and values. There are many executives and hiring managers who volunteer their time this way.

4. Spread the news of your reputation through others. Let them promote you! It's not who you know – it's who knows you!

CHAPTER 7

PUTTING THE 4P'S INTO ACTION – SETTING GOALS FOR YOUR FUTURE

"All progress takes place outside the comfort zone."
—Michael John Bobak

Once you've found a position that meets your current needs, does the search end?

No! If you want to continue moving up the ladder, the hunt is a continuous process until you retire.

After the process of losing my job and finding a new one, I vowed to never be in a situation where I wasn't in control of my career path. I developed a set of goals and a company profile for the types of job that I wanted to have. This job would combine my professional skill, my love for travel, my volunteer life and the opportunity to grow in the organization.

My goals were:

- **Salary:** Increase my income at least $25K per year in salary, bonuses, and incentives
- **Position:** Director or VP of an Enterprise Project Management Office
- **Travel**: A position offering international travel opportunities
- **Headquarters:** Northeast, Mid-Atlantic or Southeast U.S.
- **Work from Home**: The capability for me and my teams to work from a home-based office as needed
- **Benefits:** Medical/dental, mobile phone, three weeks' vacation, 401K match program

Your goals will look different than mine, but it is important to set them *before* you're looking for a job. Aligning your goals with specific opportunities allows you to avoid wasting time appealing to organizations that aren't a good fit for your needs.

Typically, I have progressed positions every 2-3 years. Each time I do, I create a new set of goals for the next position I would like to move into.

DEVELOPING A PLAN

To reach a goal, you must develop a plan. The first thing you need to do is determine your location preferences. There's no point in applying to a job in Dallas if you know you must stay in California. Create a geographical radius you're willing to apply in and don't go beyond it–unless you want to or are willing to move.

Write out exactly what you want from a job from most important to least important. Consider what will be most impactful to your life, and items that you are negotiable on. Here are a few things many people don't consider:

Intrinsic Benefits:

- Company Culture
- Parental Leave
- Path to Promotion
- Organization Hierarchy
- Company Reputation
- Company Stability
- Daily Tasks

Extrinsic Benefits:

- Vacation Time
- Flex Time
- Parental Leave
- Internet Policy
- Commute Time

MATCHING UP

In my search, it was important to determine if my salary goals and the desired positions matched. I pulled as many job descriptions as I could find, cross-referenced the requirements, and developed a list of common skills that were needed for the positions. Next, I determined the skills that I had and did a gap analysis to discover what I was missing.

In my case, I needed the following:

- Manage a portfolio of $50M in projects or more
- Management of at least 5 people reporting directly to me
- Building up of PMO's from scratch

Now that I'd determined my gaps, I developed a gap plan and executed it for the next two years. Specifically, I made an effort to seek new venues for continuing education, did on the job training for new portfolio management tools, and requested more responsibility over large projects.

I then determined what companies I wanted to pursue and pulled up census data on companies whose headquarters were in Pennsylvania, New Jersey, and Delaware. I crossed-referenced these companies with BDPA-sponsored companies and names of people with whom I had a personal connection. This yielded approximately 10 companies. From these companies, I executed the 4P's to get my desired job and position.

A few questions to ask yourself:

- What skills do you need to move up the ladder?
- Who can help you gain those skills?
- Where do you have (or where can you create) personal connections that can be leveraged later?

EXECUTING THE 4P'S

Building the Product

I got my resume in order, but more importantly, I created a proposal for hiring me as a Project Management Office Director. I wrote the proposal using a business case format. The elements of the proposal contained:

- Executive Summary
- The Opportunity (for the company) – My value proposition
- The case for having a PMO
- The scope of responsibilities and the proposed size of the team
- My value proposition detailed
- Career Summary
- Project Schedule (From the day of the proposal to the hiring date and 100 days after). I used this to show my project and organization skills. I hit each date including offer letter, acceptance and start date on target. This was added at the end of each proposal after I met with a colleague or prospective employer.

Before I finalized the proposal, I sent it to my personal *board of directors*. These contacts were from a group called the League of Executive African-American Professionals (LEAAP) I had co-formed a few years before. It was literally founded on the golf course, where a few of my executive friends got together a couple times a year. We decided to be each other's support network for upward career movement. Through the years, this group has been an invaluable resource to me. In this case, the group helped hone my leadership experience to create a stronger proposal.

To see the details of the proposal – you can access www.cljassoc.com/jobsearchbook.

Finding Promoters

Now that I had my proposal and resume together, I went on a campaign with people who could promote me. I called up people that worked at each of the 10 companies and arranged dinner/drinks/coffee. I also asked them to read my proposal. This allowed me to get feedback, as well as have a better understanding of what their company needed. After the meetings, I personally followed up with each one of these connections.

Positioning Myself

For a major role that I was being recruited for, the positioning was established years before I did an interview. Thanks to one of my "promoter" meetings, I got a phone call from a CIO asking if their HR department could contact me. This resulted in a panel interview with three individuals, but the CIO opted out of interviewing me himself. He had known me for several years and already knew he wanted to hire me-- the panel interview was just a matter of logistics. In a sense, I had the job before the company even contacted me. They were already aware of my skill set and accomplishments, I just had to show interest.

Naming the Price

Once the interview process was done, the company reached out to me an offered a job. However, I didn't accept it on the spot. Instead, I ensured the benefits lined up with my original goals and countered their salary offer. I not only secured the job but landed a salary above the median for the position. I got a $35,000 lift in total compensation over my previous job and got every single prerequisite I put on my original goals list. I also got the title I was seeking--

Director of the Project Management Office. Overall the process to meet my goals took more than two years, but I couldn't have asked for a better fit.

IF YOU'RE JUST STARTING

Much of this book is addressed to working professionals who already have some experience under their belts. If you're at the start of your career journey, keep this book around. Many of the concepts will hold true in future years as you begin your climb up the career ladder.

However, if you're at the start of your working career, don't discount the fact that you can take small actions **right now** that will have an enormous impact in the coming years. No matter what position you're in at this point, you can always provide your company value by modeling yourself after the Three R's: Respectful, Responsible, Reliable.

If you have a low-end job, you have the advantage of longevity. Most minimum-wage jobs have a very high employee turnover rate, which can be used to your advantage. By simply showing up on time, taking on tasks others avoid, and being respectful to your customers and coworkers, you are already two steps ahead of your peers. You can rise to the top quickly and create value for your company because they don't have to spend money to replace you.

The Three R's also apply when you take on your first career-related position. Although you may not have much decision-making power at the onset, managing relationships is the key to forward momentum. Your superiors will inevitably leave, move up, or retire at some point, so you should position yourself to take on their responsibilities by building trust. When they like you, they'll trust you. When they trust you, they'll share knowledge freely.

CHAPTER 7 ACTION ITEMS

1. Set goals for what you want and where you want it.

2. Develop a plan to achieve those goals.

3. Narrow down your search as much as possible. Be specific about your career opportunity

4. Find what you want and use all your resources to go after it.

CHAPTER 8

PAY IT FORWARD: SUCCESS STORIES

"You can have everything you want in life if you just help enough people get what they want in life." —Zig Ziglar

Why am I confident that marketing yourself properly gets you the job? I see this process in action every single day. I have helped hundreds of people achieve success by marketing themselves over the last 15 years. This is a labor of love that I want to do as long as I am alive. My personal vision is to change my world one person at a time. Whenever someone that I help benefits, I am changing my world and getting a new friend for life. Here are just a few stories.

Suzette's Story

Suzette was an IT professional who had been out of work for over a couple of years. She was being passed over by employers because of the gap in her resume created by her starting a family. The rejection had a negative impact on her self-confidence.

During her search, her husband was in a major accident. Suddenly, the job hunt that was mildly frustrating became an urgent situation. She needed a job quickly. Every step seemed like an uphill battle as she dealt with mounting living expenses and a quest to find meaningful work. Nothing was going her direction.

The changes we made were small. I simply helped her reformat her resume to cover the gaps of time she was unemployed and put the resume on a special paper that had a uniquely orange hue. All Suzette needed was a boost of confidence and a way to stand out from all the other applicants. I asked her:

- To identify what she wanted to do in the future, and distinguish that from what she did in the past.
- To package herself as a product by changing her resume to be more functional and tailored to her capabilities while eliminating the employment timeline.

- To improve her interview skills, specifically her word choice in describing her contributions and capabilities.

The small changes made a big difference. One hiring manager even commented that they had never seen a resume formatted with an orange hue before. Now, I don't suggest everyone change their resume color. But in this situation, it was a change that literally stood out in a pile of papers and got her to the interview stage.

Suzette took this advice to heart and was offered the job after the interview. She did not get this job through a referral, or by knowing the hiring manager, but because of her newfound self-confidence, and her increased ability to understand and sell herself to the hiring managers.

She said this about the process:

"Curtis worked with me to highlight my brand and show that I am a product. Each time I submit my resume, I'm selling myself to the person who is reviewing it. I was able to communicate that I am a person who can "get the job done," and that I'm the "best available" candidate for the job, and a valued asset to any company. I was able to secure

the first job I applied for after being laid off for almost 2 years! With my updated resume, I was able to assist others with securing employment using the same resume editing format and interviewing practice techniques."

Sharon's Story

Sharon was a good friend of my wife's. She was a teaching assistant who had been out of work for a long time. As a single mom, she was at wits' end as she struggled to get her kids through high school. Her confidence was really low and it showed. Life had beaten her down.

All I did was give her knowledge. It was a purely psychological change that needed to occur. I told her to write a story about herself as if she had her dream job. We linked the story to her negative self-perception. Over a few sessions, she gained an enormous amount of confidence. This confidence was furthered by her attending job fairs and a number of interviews. She got an offer for the second position she interviewed for.

Lawrence's Story

Lawrence was a superior of mine. As a contractor at

Amtrak, he held an enormous amount of influence regarding people and budgets. Although he was happy in his position, he couldn't find the upward mobility he wanted. Since he was already known as a guru in the information security industry, I convinced him to rebuild his resume with the most important parts distilled. The revised resume highlighted his leadership and industry knowledge. He immediately secured a better a job at a top consulting firm using his new resume.

He said this about the process:

"I had the skills to grow my career, however, I didn't know how to put it on paper. I needed help to pull that information out of me. Curtis helped me focus my thoughts. He had me truly think about what I was looking to do with my career. He was able to place the information I provided him during our work sessions into a resume form. Once I put that resume out on several executive job sites, I immediately received several responses. It assured me that I made the correct choice in working with Curtis. After we completed the process, I had the format to provide the perfect resume for any job or opportunity I would be looking to go after. I now have the skill set to determine if any opportunity I am looking at does truly align with my personal roadmap. I have solidified my

professional brand truly understanding my worth."

Leslie's* Story

In 2009, my company was being bought by another company. At that time, there were several employees who were asked to stay, and some who were asked to leave. I was one of the fortunate ones asked to stay. My co-worker Leslie was asked to leave. She struggled with why she got the boot while I didn't.

"I know as many people as you know, and I have done as many projects as you," she said. As I thought about my reply, I realized that she was making a couple of faulty comparisons. The first was that we were equal in the number of people in our network as determined by our LinkedIn connections. The second was in the exact number of projects she delivered versus the exact number of projects that I delivered.

The first thing I did was help her understand the context of our comparisons. I started with the comparison on projects by asking her a very simple question, "At the end of the year during the CIOs

---

* name changed

presentation on projects, whose projects are highlighted?" It was then she realized that I was right and that my projects had global visibility and her projects did not. I asked her if she took every single project that she was asked to manage, and she said yes. I told her I only take on projects that have a high degree of visibility and in this case these projects were mergers and acquisitions. She asked me if I had ever turned down a project when requested, and I told her I did. The aha moment for her was that it was clear that I was in control of my career and that she was just executing projects that were not seen as high value and high visibility to the company.

I helped her revise her LinkedIn profile and resume. She knew as many people as I did, but her recommendations came from a single month, which didn't show a history of providing value. Together, we were able to work together to secure her next job as a contractor and project manager.

BEING A SERVANT LEADER

Nothing gives me more satisfaction than helping someone get a good job. Over the last 15+ years, I have helped many people find the confidence needed to continue developing their careers. By helping others use the principles of the Four P's to advance their own careers, I found that I opened doors for myself in several different ways.

Below are a few more testimonials from people who have successfully used my techniques and coaching.

TESTIMONIALS/CASES

1. Brocklin Gaither—Looking for career growth:

"Curtis Jenkins was able to take my existing resume and turn it into a concise, focused one. As this was for a hands-on technical position, he made sure to focus my resume on the appropriate skills and work history. This enabled my resume to get the attention it deserved and led me to my current employment which I have been engaged with for six years. I am extremely grateful for his efforts and career advice."

2. Loren Fanroy — Wanted to move up into management/leadership:

"I came to Curtis hoping to revamp my resume as a recent college graduate wanting to highlight her key

accomplishments, having been in the professional world for about a year and a half at the time. He helped me completely redesign my resume and write out all accomplishments and skills from a results–based perspective. Since then, I have received many compliments on how thorough and impressive my resume is. I truly think Curtis helped me reflect who I am as a brand on a piece of paper. It has helped me tell the story of my background with ease and thorough detail in a way that would be attractive to anyone receiving my resume. Would HIGHLY recommend!"

3. Brian Rodgers — Out of work for one year; got a job as a manager at a major business store:

"I can't describe how much I appreciate this! Now that we've spoken it's really opened my eyes to this, and just this little advice you've given me has been very beneficial. I will get all this done right away, because it will be vital to me landing a great position."

4. Brandon Bennett — Student looking to get a job for the first time:

"Prior to receiving help with my resume, I didn't have any sense of direction of where to start. I had used a few

different Google templates but those were very basic and looked amateur. After having my resume redone, it gave me a greater sense of confidence in applying for jobs. Now it is very easy to make alterations to my resume because I have the professional structure. I also got a job with the updated resume that I am currently still working for today."

CHAPTER 8 ACTION ITEMS

1. Mentor others to increase your network.

2. Helping someone else get a job is a huge confidence booster. Help someone while you are also looking for a job.

3. Make connecting others your life's work—always be of service.

4. Don't ever give up on a job search that may seem impossible.

A FINAL NOTE

My method of helping you gain the job you want is deliberate in the sense that it requires you to change your behavior when necessary while acting in the face of the risk of failure. You can't help how hiring managers behave and there will be times that you become frustrated with how long someone takes to get back to you—if they get back to you at all. When you witness or experience bad behavior, you have been given a gift. That gift is having avoided a person or company that is not aligned with the type of culture that you are seeking. Don't despair; keep your dignity. Do not go onto social media or other platforms to bash the company or their employee(s). Just continue to follow the processes to ensure you are using the Marketing Mix of Product, Price, Promotion, and Place/Position to your benefit. Keep your skills relevant and take advantage of all the opportunities to educate yourself in your field.

These methods are also not limited to job search, but in anything that you seek. It comes down to an exchange between human beings. The brand is how people see you, not how you see yourself. The network and the willingness of others to hire you, promote you, and help you be in the best position is very important to have whether you are searching for a job, trying to sell a product, seeking a promotion, or teaching a course. Use the Marketing Mix to help show the value that you possess in a way that is attractive to others – to give you what you desire. Stay positive and I guarantee it will happen for you.

ACKNOWLEDGMENTS

My family encouraged me to write this book. I put together details of my actions relative to job searching in order to help a family friend's husband. He asked how I had found a job so fast and went on to say that he had been job searching for over a year. This book evolved out of this request for help. In subsequent years, Cheryl developed a course to help young women in their job search, and I helped her by suggesting the same techniques to help them find gainful employment.

Thanks are also due to my brothers in the League of Executive African-American Professionals (LEAAP). LEAAP, a group which I co-founded, is a group of men who support each other as a personal board of directors. These men are always there for me and are true to LEAAP's mission of developing the members' leadership skills, and helping each other become better leaders, businessmen, husbands, and fathers. LEAAP works through education, idea exchange, peer support, and peer accountability. I have been blessed to have helped my LEAAP brothers' friends and family members find, or get better, jobs.

In the wake of his company's impending divestiture, Claude Demby, the other co-founder of the group, asked me for a consolidated document of tips and techniques which he could use to help people on the verge of losing their jobs. I realized that I didn't have the new/updated information that I had learned since the first draft in 2002, and that I needed to put the information together in a consumable format. This was also a sign that I needed to write this book and develop my online course.

I want to acknowledge the hundreds of people who gave me the opportunity to fulfill my values and vision by taking on the techniques described in this book, including those who gave me a written testimony on their experiences. These people are now happy and growing in their careers because they were willing to take effective actions and develop the confidence needed to make themselves stand out in their search for employment.

Finally, I want to acknowledge my network of close social and professional friends who have helped me to shape my thoughts with their feedback on this book. The advice was very good and helped me to shape this book into a reference guide so that anyone can follow the actions to gain confidence in their job search and career.

QUESTIONS TO HELP YOU WITH YOUR 4P'S

Product

1. What type of product are you?

2. What is the headline to describe you and how you are better than all of the other products out there?

3. Why are you the best product and why should someone buy you and your skills?

4. What is it that you want?

5. What does the job you want look like?

6. Does your resume answer all the questions I asked above? If not, there is work to do as you now have to establish your "brand."

7. Discuss your network with me. Can your current surrounding of friends, family, and professional colleagues help you to achieve your goals?

8. Who do you spend the most time with outside of your immediate family, and are they progressive people who can help you?

9. Finally, we need to discuss your job accomplishments. Your resume should speak of how you resolve problems, innovate, or create.

Price

1. What are you worth?
2. Why are you worth this?
3. Are you worth more?
4. What evidence do you have that you are worth more?
5. What do you think people are willing to pay?

Place

1. Where do you want to work?
2. Do you have global experience?
3. Where have you been and where do you want to be?

Promotion

1. Can your network get you where you want to be?
2. Do you have a big network or people that will promote your skills?
3. What do people say about you that you don't say about yourself?

SUMMARY OF ACTIONS

Chapter 1: Get Moving; Take Action

- Reject Shame. Do not be embarrassed that you lost your job.
- Apply for unemployment.
- Develop a routine and refine it as required.
- Pay for what you need to get what you want.
- Step out of your comfort zone.

Chapter 2: Using the 4P's of Marketing to Sell Yourself

- Read and understand marketing in terms of the 4P's.
- Make sure that you can answer these personal marketing questions:
  - Product – What are you selling?
  - Place – Are you in the right place, business, profession, industry, position?
  - Promotion – How is your brand/image – What do people say about you?
  - Price – What value do you bring?

- Continuously refine the answers to these personal marketing questions while on your job search.

Chapter 3: Product Development in Action

- Get your resume in order. Look at current examples of great resumes in your field of work. Have it reviewed by trustworthy and skilled colleagues.
- Prepare for the interview like you would prepare for a huge test.
- Practice interviewing with trusted colleagues, family members, mentors, sponsors, etc.
- Develop a marketing proposal for hiring you and use it after the interview.
- Always follow-up from interviews as you would do with any new potential relationship.

Chapter 4: Getting the Right Price for you as a Product

- Know your value based on research. Use available tools such as salary.com and payscale.com to help you with your research.
- Know your value based on your experience and

accomplishments. Consult with peers/ colleagues to help you best express your value.

- Study salary negotiations skills and techniques. Use the list of nine points to help you.

Chapter 5: Are You in the Right Place or Position?

- How can you put yourself in a "buy-level" position? Look at your past and current position – are you ready for a growth opportunity?
- Ask for what you want. Determine what you want to do and ask people of influence to help you.
- Develop a list of people who would be great mentors or, better yet, sponsors. Determine who can make introductions or sponsor you.

Chapter 6: Promotion – By Others

- Don't wait until you need a network before trying to create one. Start now, whether you are employed or not.
- Attend networking events and actively seek out the right people for mutually beneficial relationships.

- Assume a highly-visible position of authority with an affinity group/association.
- Spread the news of your reputation through others. Let them promote you!

Chapter 7: Putting the 4P's into action: Setting goals for your future

- Set goals for what you want and where you want it.
- Develop a plan to achieve the goals.
- Narrow down your search as much as possible. Be specific about your career opportunity.
- Find what you want and use all your resources to go after it.

Chapter 8: Pay It Forward

- Mentor others to increase your network.
- Helping someone else get a job is a huge confidence booster. Help someone while you are also looking for a job.
- Make connecting others your life's work— always be of service.

- Don't ever give up on a job search that may seem impossible.

WEBSITES USEFUL TO THE JOB SEEKER

Here are some of the online job websites that I used during my search.

www.Ladders.com

www.jobcircle.com

www.monster.com

www.computerjobs.com

www.linkedin.com

www.indeed.com

www.dice.com

www.glassdoor.com

PERSONALITY TYPES – MYERS BRIGGS

There are 16 Personality types. Learn yours by taking the Myers Briggs Personality Test. It will provide insight into how you can leverage your personality to shape how you take action and build your confidence. The personality types and descriptions are:

1. ISTJ: The Duty Fulfiller - Serious and quiet, interested in security and peaceful living. Extremely thorough, responsible, and dependable. Well-developed powers of concentration. Usually interested in supporting and promoting traditions and establishments. Well-organized and hardworking, they work steadily towards identified goals. They can usually accomplish any task once they have set their mind to it.

2. ISTP: The Mechanic - Quiet and reserved, interested in how and why things work. Excellent skills with mechanical things. Risk-takers who they live for the moment. Usually interested in and

talented at extreme sports. Uncomplicated in their desires. Loyal to their peers and to their internal value systems, but not overly concerned with respecting laws and rules if they get in the way of getting something done. Detached and analytical, they excel at finding solutions to practical problems.

3. ISFJ: The Nurturer - Quiet, kind, and conscientious. Can be depended on to follow through. Usually puts the needs of others above their own needs. Stable and practical, they value security and traditions. Well-developed sense of space and function. Rich inner world of observations about people. Extremely perceptive of other's feelings. Interested in serving others.

4. ISFP: The Artist - Quiet, serious, sensitive and kind. Do not like conflict, and not likely to do things which may generate conflict. Loyal and faithful. Extremely well-developed senses, and aesthetic appreciation for beauty. Not interested in leading or controlling others. Flexible and open-minded. Likely to be original and creative. Enjoy the present moment.

5. INFJ: The Protector - Quietly forceful, original,

and sensitive. Tend to stick to things until they are done. Extremely intuitive about people and concerned for their feelings. Well-developed value systems which they strictly adhere to. Well-respected for their perseverance in doing the right thing. Likely to be individualistic, rather than leading or following.

6. INFP: The Idealist - Quiet, reflective, and idealistic. Interested in serving humanity. Well-developed value system, which they strive to live in accordance with. Extremely loyal. Adaptable and laid-back unless a strongly-held value is threatened. Usually talented writers. Mentally quick, and able to see possibilities. Interested in understanding and helping people.

7. INTJ: The Scientist - Independent, original, analytical, and determined. Have an exceptional ability to turn theories into solid plans of action. Highly value knowledge, competence, and structure. Driven to derive meaning from their visions. Long-range thinkers. Have very high standards for their performance, and the performance of others. Natural leaders but will follow if they trust existing leaders.

8. INTP: The Thinker - Logical, original, creative thinkers. Can become very excited about theories and ideas. Exceptionally capable and driven to turn theories into clear understandings. Highly value knowledge, competence and logic. Quiet and reserved, hard to get to know well. Individualistic, having no interest in leading or following others.

9. ESTP: The Doer - Friendly, adaptable, action-oriented. "Doers" who are focused on immediate results. Living in the here-and-now, they're risk-takers who live fast-paced lifestyles. Impatient with long explanations. Extremely loyal to their peers, but not usually respectful of laws and rules if they get in the way of getting things done. Great people skills.

10. ESTJ: The Guardian - Practical, traditional, and organized. Likely to be athletic. Not interested in theory or abstraction unless they see the practical application. Have clear visions of the way things should be. Loyal and hard-working. Like to be in charge. Exceptionally capable in organizing and running activities. "Good citizens" who value security and peaceful living.

11. ESFP: The Performer - People-oriented and fun-

loving, they make things more fun for others by their enjoyment. Living for the moment, they love new experiences. They dislike theory and impersonal analysis. Interested in serving others. Likely to be the center of attention in social situations. Well-developed common sense and practical ability.

12. ESFJ: The Caregiver - Warm-hearted, popular, and conscientious. Tend to put the needs of others over their own needs. Feel strong sense of responsibility and duty. Value traditions and security. Interested in serving others. Need positive reinforcement to feel good about themselves. Well-developed sense of space and function.

13. ENFP: The Inspirer - Enthusiastic, idealistic, and creative. Able to do almost anything that interests them. Great people skills. Need to live life in accordance with their inner values. Excited by new ideas but bored with details. Open-minded and flexible, with a broad range of interests and abilities.

14. ENFJ: The Giver - Popular and sensitive, with outstanding people skills. Externally focused, with real concern for how others think and feel. Usually

dislike being alone. They see everything from the human angle, and dislike impersonal analysis. Very effective at managing people issues, and leading group discussions. Interested in serving others, and probably place the needs of others over their own needs.

15. ENTP: The Visionary - Creative, resourceful, and intellectually quick. Good at a broad range of things. Enjoy debating issues and may be into "one-upmanship." They get very excited about new ideas and projects but may neglect the more routine aspects of life. Generally outspoken and assertive. They enjoy people and are stimulating company. Excellent ability to understand concepts and apply logic to find solutions.

16. ENTJ: The Executive - Assertive and outspoken - they are driven to lead. Excellent ability to understand difficult organizational problems and create solid solutions. Intelligent and well-informed, they usually excel at public speaking. They value knowledge and competence, and usually have little patience with inefficiency or disorganization.